Praise for

Mid-Life Poetry

An invitation to climb the trails at life's halfway point

"Powerful, poignant and even playful at times! Kerstin has crafted her words into a real, relatable page-turner that evokes unchartered thoughts, inspiration and a range of emotions throughout. What a great way to relay to others — you are never alone on this journey!"

- Tiffany Hicks, Artist

"It was just like sitting down with you and chatting. Thank you for giving me the privilege to read this delightful book."

- Lynne Fox, Entrepreneur

"Kerstin's work is bold, honest, and makes my soul sing. She delightfully captures this whimsical time of life we all must endure and provides a dash of companionship so we know that we don't have to go it alone!"

- Kimberley Schumacher,
Founder Avallon's Voice

Kerstin, this is a lovely collection capturing your authentic vulnerable self. I greatly appreciate the privilege to be brought into your inner world. It was a precious gift."

- Linda Christiansen, Artist

"Kerstin's words are honest and so relatable. I found myself reflecting, yearning and feeling everything from sadness to laughing out loud. It's refreshing to know that we're not alone and we all have those "experiences" that form our lives. Thanks Kerstin, for giving me a reason to pause and reflect for just a little while!"

- Marianne Ashton, Life Traveler

www.midlifepoetry.net

First Printing 2021

ISBN: 978-1-7923-2620-2

Printed in the United States of America

Mid-Life Poetry

An invitation to climb the trails

at life's halfway point

with

Kerstin Schaefer

Dear CJ,

Thank you for staying true to who you are so we get to share the beautiful person you are!

Love,

Kerstin M. Schaefer

In Honor of my mom,

who, my whole life through,

was the best example of love

and what it means to be a woman of strength.

And to the man who loved her.

Acknowledgements

This book is a collaboration of many. Everyone who reviewed and proof read this
material had encouraging insights and inspiring reactions to share.
The ride is smoother on this road of life with friends and guides around us.

Kimberley, I thank you for your unfailing, ever present love and support.
You encourage me to be better, to do more. Your artful talent to keep me on my path is
appreciated beyond words!

Tiffany, I adore your loving heart and your true spirit. Your input is invaluable and your
creative eye is simply amazing. My days are brighter because of you in my life, Sila!

Thank you, Deb, Jenni, Kath, Linda, Lolita, Lynne and Marianne!
Your gifts of time have humbled me and your courage to express your honest feedback has
broadened my horizon and challenged me in the best way possible.

Claudia, I admire your adventurous spirit and excursions. Your love of nature and
interpretation through your photography is a beautiful thing. Thank you for letting me be a
part of it.

Thanks to the Lord for the inspiration for this book, for surrounding me with wonderful and
supportive people and for giving me the courage to share my thoughts.

To my fellow Mid-Life Season Travelers,

As I started to reflect on my challenges of this crisis/menopause/mom of a teenager season and talked with my friends about theirs, it became evident that, even though we go our own way, we all walk in the same direction.

This book is a winding trail into my thoughts and feelings during this time. It is meant to bring you comfort and companionship no matter where you are on your travels.

I hope my words make you curious, bring tears to your eyes and laughter to your heart.

Most of all I wish for you to be encouraged. You ARE able to get through this time of life and should be proud of who you are becoming and re-discovering.

I invite you to slow down with me as we explore this amazing adventure of ours together.

It is a delight to have you along,

Kerstin

TABLE OF
CONTENTS

Growing Up

(Read from bottom to top)

YIKES!

AM.

I

HERE

YET

DO.

TO

THING

EASY

AN

NOT

IS

50

AT

UP

GROWING

TRAIL
MARKER

Throughout our lives it is not only we who change and grow, but also the people around us.

As we get older our perspective changes.

The relationship between my father and I has had many seasons. It has taken work, time, endurance, and love to develop it to where it is today.

Now, as he is happily sharing his love and insights, filled with all the knowledge and wisdom learned along the way, I am taking it all in eagerly and reveling in this very precious gift of his legacy.

"I appreciate how it makes me think of my parents, yet also makes me think of how my relationship is changing with my kids."

- Lynne F.

The Gift

für Papa

Humbly given and joyfully received.

Surrounded by beauty, that spark, that voice of life.

Once loud and wild with Oh, so many questions.

Now calm and quiet, filled with knowledge and love.

How can I help you?

What do you need?

I'm here.

I'm here.

Let go your sorrows, lift up your eyes.

Give me your ear, your heart for just a little while.

I live to serve, to love, to laugh.

Today, tomorrow, 'til time has passed.

An offering - so pure

Joyfully given and humbly received.

TRAIL
MARKER

This is my truth, my reality, my season. Reading these comments, it looks like some of my readers are experiencing the same as I:

Light with heavy content

Powerful and to the point!   **YES!**

Honest   Transparent

Relatable   Hard   Real

Whimsically challenging

"This made me laugh out loud... so much said in a few words."

- a friend UpNorth

THE TRIFECTA

Midlife Crisis
Menopause
Millennial Teenager

Translates into an

Everchanging
Highly Emotional
Utterly confused

Woman

TRAIL
MARKER

Topsy turvy comes to mind when I think about the responses to midlife crises.

At times we just can't tell which side is up anymore.

As for my part, I started reflecting and going back to my roots, as well as exploring new things.

All of us are so unique that there is a variety of ways one can react to these years of change.

Looking at the list, I guess I'd be the chimpanzee!

Figures! Leave it up to me to be the monkey!

"I found myself relating to more than one animal!

I love how playful the words are... it's a realization of how we cope in life."

- T. H.

Climacteric Animal Comparison

Choose one of these and laugh, if you can. You may be woman, you may be man:

Are you the *Gorilla*? Just make sure it's not gonna kill ya,

working out and gaining muscle, hustle-hustle-hustle.

Maybe you're the *Cheetah*? Cruising with your señorita,

needing the speed, buying fast cars with no limits to heed.

How about a *Donkey*? Keeping everything low key,

slowing down and just relaxing might be to others very vexing.

Possibly the *Chimpanzee*? Going down in history,

for learning new things and ready to explore. To be sung about in many a folklore.

You could be a *Wildebeest*! Which will, not to say the least,

travel hundreds of miles and has the most 'moving' of lifestyles.

Or are you hiding like a *Mole*? Staying deep within your hole,

hardly leaving your home. Not even for this poem.

I hope you're not an *Octopus*, and aren't making too much fuss!

Changing your moods, swinging back and forth. Maybe you should move Up North?

There are a few more I could think of

But the list, this list above

Shows directions we may go

To cope with our years of woe

In the end we must stay true

and find our "inner You"

Whatever that choice

Whatever that voice

Once balanced again after all the strife

We find in this glorious scheme of life

We are meant to become

And isn't it quite the fun ?!?

TRAIL
MARKER

Sleep does not come easy these days.
Sitting in the dark with a steaming cup of tea, I admire the cold stillness outside and wait for the day to begin.
Venus sits high in the sky on this beautiful December morning and reminds me of the small, yet important, part I play in our universe.
As the sun starts to peek out from behind the houses, people are awakening and preparing for a brand new day.
What will it have in store?
Grateful, I am anticipating the adventures ahead.

"I love that this morning's sunrise does not define itself by last night's sunset."

- Steve Maraboli

Morning Anticipation

Daytime is dawning

Competing with homes alight

Young and old yawning

The new day looks bright

Schedules to keep

Throughout the day

While the hours creep

We'll go our way

Later we shall return as before

To our warm dwelling

And close the door

As the night comes felling

This day

Lights go on

And we're pleased that we may

Reflect on what was done

Then reconnect with the people we love

Once more

The night rises above

And we realize all that we have and are grateful for

TRAIL MARKER

A most amazing spectacle!

The first snow! We can't help but stare as it comes down in droves and we eagerly look forward to stepping out onto this glistening blanket.

The first snow! The beauty is breathtaking. Our neighbors have become our comrades in arms as we all shovel and blow the snow into hills.

The first snow! For a little while, everything else just stops in its tracks. We can forget about our challenges and fears and simply focus on this illuminating shower.

"Playful and soft - Makes snow feel like a good friend."

- Sila

Snow

And snow it begins

We stop and stare

And watch in wonder

Breathing in

The change in season

Kids roll in it

Grown ups find their laugh

And Lovers slide closer

Coming together

We form a bond in harmony

Watching

As snowflakes descend

To find their home

And settle in

Sharing their voyage

with us

TRAIL
MARKER

Give yourself permission to stop and smell the roses.

Breathe in deeply.

Feel the sunshine warm your body.

Be refreshed.

"Felt peaceful ... love is everywhere."

- Kathy

Love

The sky opens and lets through a most delicious ray of sunshine

It warms every particle in my body

and covers my skin with an enormous amount of delightful kisses

The air smells like home and is carried about by the slightest breeze

Love resides here

Feel it

And let it be felt

TRAIL MARKER

For his 13th birthday we bought our son a dog. He really wanted one and my husband was all for it. I was the one having to get used to the idea.

For a few months I could only see the added stress the animal brought into our home and that we were losing our freedoms by needing to take care of him.

Then I decided to change my perspective and the little furry pup grew on me.

Now, I love having him around. He's always happy to see me and helps me get through the toughest of times.

"Money can buy you a fine dog, but only love can make him wag his tail."

- Kinky Friedman

THE Dog

You were so cute when you arrived,

but something just did not seem right

I was unsure that you belonged,

the cuteness helped, don't get me wrong

You persevered and always loved

for three long years—oh, heaven above

And now I watch you as you trot

so joyfully across the lot

Then sitting there in black and white

What a curious little sight

Looking like a prince-per-chance

Showing off your majestical stance

It's time to say 'I love you too'

How loyal and how very true

You have turned out to be

And this is very much the key

To change your name

and highly proclaim

For others to know

You are **MY** dog

And that's just so!

TRAIL
MARKER

Whether you are a mother, a grandmother, a sister, a daughter, an aunt, or a friend, along the trails of life we will find ourselves in a position where our help, our insights, and sometimes our love is rejected.
It is very hard to watch people we love choose to walk in darkness for a while.

There is hurt.

There is pain.

And then there is LOVE.

"One thorn of experience is worth a whole wilderness of warning."

- James Russell Lowell

My Love

Your road ahead is tough

and one I've left behind

It is by choice

my choice

to love

to watch your battles

and wait, patiently

until you find

your way

your road

to rise above

Then I'll be there

with helping hands

to pull you up

out of that hole

To love you

and to help you mend

that lonely

desperate soul

TRAIL
MARKER

When we are overwhelmed, all kinds of feelings can surface.

Feelings that need to go somewhere.

Sometimes we try hard to be stoic and hold back the tears.

But why?

What do we need to prove?

It can be a great relief, cleansing even, to shed some tears.

"It's ok to cry, the sky does it too."

- Unknown

Tears

Tears

will come.

Let them come.

They cleanse, they

matter. They are joy and

sorrow, hope and regret. They

show you feel, and feel so dearly.

So, let them flow. And when they've

dried, take in the brightness and

rest in the calm, that grows

from being watered by all

those precious

tears.

TRAIL
MARKER

"Truth! If everything in life came easy, we would not grow and would most likely take things for granted!"

- A wise reader

"Good advice!"

- Lolita M.

Obstacles

Treat your challenges like adventures

and they might just turn out to be

the most rewarding experiences

along your road.

TRAIL
MARKER

Not too long ago, I was traveling through an emotional dark valley. I seemed to have taken some wrong turns along the way and was rather lost.

The person I had become was a stranger to me.

Little by little, I am carving the real me out from under all kinds of self-deception, expectations, regrets, and confusion.

It is amazing to find the 'old me' again here and there.

Occasionally I even get a glimpse of the 'future me'.

"Not until we are lost do we begin to understand ourselves."

- Henry David Thoreau

Homecoming

I'm home

I am the person I'm supposed to be

The feeling overwhelms me

Starting a fire within my soul

Moving to my mind and through my body

Until it reaches all my fingers and toes

I want to BE this forever

Alas, it takes to the air and flies away

Lingering behind is the solid promise

That it will return

Next time, I will hold on to it a little longer

And even longer the time after that

Until it becomes my anchor and stable companion

TRAIL
MARKER

We all have them! Things that clutter our minds. Things that need to be done now, later, next week, or next month.

If there are too many things in my head, it literally feels like there are open doors in need of closing.
Do you also have "open doors", "a lot of balls in the air", "too many cars on the road" or "spinning plates"?

Whatever we call it, it sure feels good when we can reduce the traffic in our heads.

"Makes me think of Dr. Seuss."

- Tiffany H.

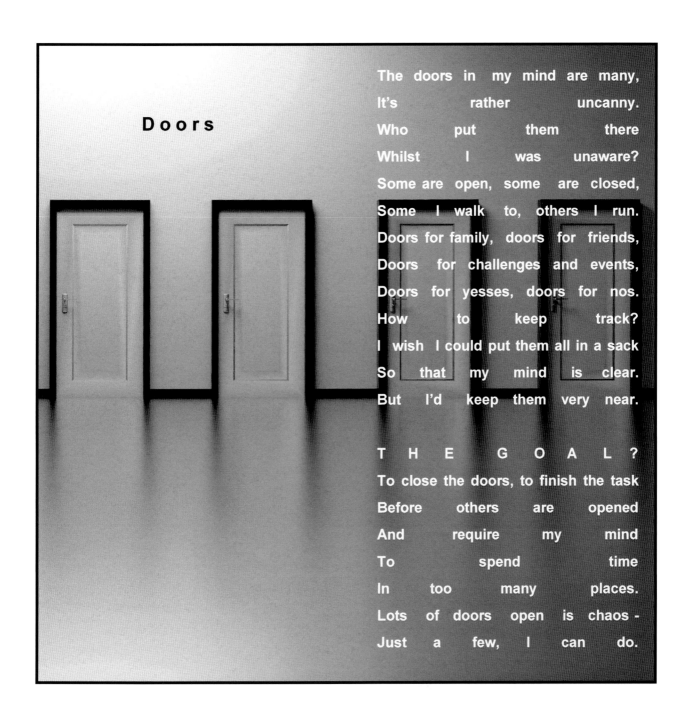

Doors

The doors in my mind are many,
It's rather uncanny.
Who put them there
Whilst I was unaware?
Some are open, some are closed,
Some I walk to, others I run.
Doors for family, doors for friends,
Doors for challenges and events,
Doors for yesses, doors for nos.
How to keep track?
I wish I could put them all in a sack
So that my mind is clear.
But I'd keep them very near.

T H E   G O A L ?
To close the doors, to finish the task
Before others are opened
And require my mind
To spend time
In too many places.
Lots of doors open is chaos -
Just a few, I can do.

TRAIL
MARKER

This is my history, my presence and my future.

At times I might find myself moving back a
couple of steps, but the end will always be the same:

Celebration

"Oh the power of words! This process can be applied to so many things! I started
plugging in different topics, then reading each of the words again..."

- A Southern Belle

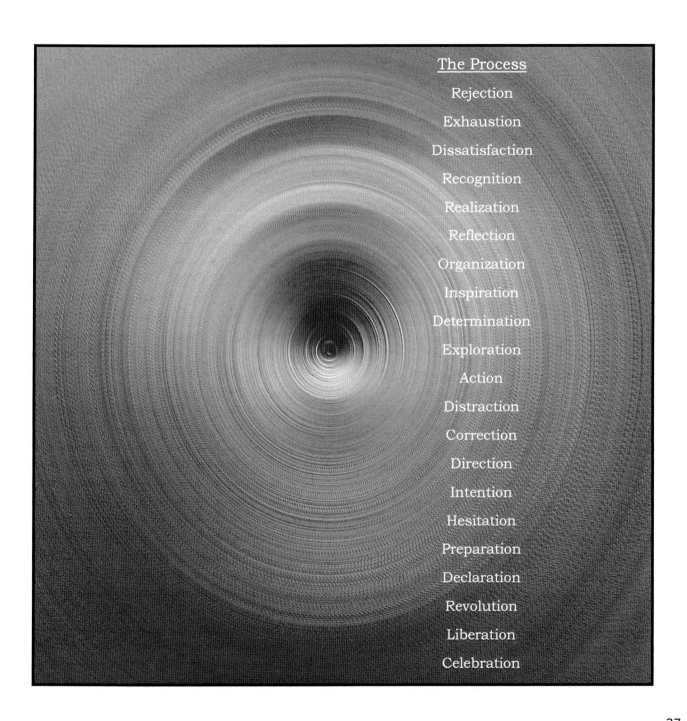

The Process

Rejection

Exhaustion

Dissatisfaction

Recognition

Realization

Reflection

Organization

Inspiration

Determination

Exploration

Action

Distraction

Correction

Direction

Intention

Hesitation

Preparation

Declaration

Revolution

Liberation

Celebration

TRAIL
MARKER

Moments can pass as quickly as they come.

To be in the moment, to truly live in the moment, is a *learned* form of art.

Listen to your heart.

There are no guarantees we will ever get the chance to experience a moment like this again.

"The best way to pay for a lovely moment is to enjoy it."

- Richard Bach

In the Moment

so quick to pass

a decision to make

grasp it, or let it go

the heart says: "take it, take it!"

the mind says: "no time, no time!"

but do, DO take it

for   in   the   moment

time   slows   down

the   heart   can   breathe

the   mind   relax

you're   in   that   place   of   no   regret

close   your   eyes   and   be   aware

there   are   no   burdens   for   you   to   bear

TRAIL
MARKER

I am looking for the young woman inside of me. The one who used to be bold, courageous, trusting and curious.
Yet she has allowed gloominess, fear and animosity enter her soul.

Being past the halfway mark on my journey, it seems she has been drowned by life itself.

But I can see the light and start to make my way to the surface by changing my perspective and searching for the good, the love.

Looking around I find myself in the company of a multitude of people on their own, yet similar, journey.

"Great message. Gratitude in action; encouraging and positive."

- K.H.

LOOK

Look for the warmth in the snow

The quiet in the noise

The gratitude in the turmoil

The peace in the tension

The love in the anger

Keep looking

Find them

And you will find yourself

Amidst the crowd

TRAIL
MARKER

Friends weave in and out of our lives.

Every single one of them touches us in one way
or another.
If in a good way, we are better because of it.

If in a challenging way, we are better because we
can learn from it.

There is a special place in my heart for a very few,
very close friends.

Here is my ode to these amazing few.

"Friendship is the only cement that will ever hold the world together."

- Woodrow T. Wilson

YOU

You are my friend,   my true, true friend.

We laugh, we cry, we disagree. We share our pains,

our hopes, our passions. This time is ours. And if our

lives take different paths, your soul, your heart,

are imprinted on my being. I thank you for

your time, and love, and thoughts,

for needing me. Because of

you I am a different,

better person.

♥

TRAIL
MARKER

I think there should be another gender: Alien!

When you're a teenager everything seems alien to you, and when you're the parent of a teenager they themselves seem alien to you.

Remembering some of my thoughts and actions when I passed through teenage-hood, makes me cringe now.
It makes me wish I'd known some things then, that I know now.

I want to help my child not to experience the same, but I can't walk his path for him. Even though at times it seems he is stepping into my very footprints.

"Your pain is the breaking of the shell that encloses your understanding."

- Khalil Gibran

Aching

I miss my mom.

And wish I'd known,

when in my younger years,

looking at her with arrogant eyes,

that it would hurt so much,

so much,

to want to be near her.

I've lost the yester years

and wish them back

to start to learn then

what I must learn now.

As now my child,

in his younger years,

Looks at me with those same eyes.

I want to yell, to scream

"I know that path!"

Yet,

would I have listened?

Back when?!?

TRAIL
MARKER

My mind is constantly filled with out-of-nowhere kind of thoughts that stay around just as brief as a firecracker exploding and fading into the night.

Recently there seem to be more of these thoughts, taking all kinds of directions.

One day, instead of letting the thoughts fade away into brain storage, I followed them.

It is worthwhile to acknowledge these whimsical thoughts; for they can make a path filled with challenges sunnier and more manageable.

"The questions which one asks oneself begin, at least, to illuminate the world, and become one's key to the experience of others."

- James Baldwin

Questions, questions...

Do elephants snore?

Does a snake ever get sore

After all that slithering and gliding?

Can a mosquito fight the wind?

Do butterflies like mint?

Oh, please, PLEASE, give me a hint!

My brain is overflowing!

Do whales ever get tired from blowing?

"Who cares?", you might ask

But you see, this is my task

To ask the questions, to find the answer

So that I can become and be aware

Of all the miracles out there!

TRAIL MARKER

There is a light at the end of the tunnel.

We will not be experiencing this change for the rest of our lives.

Be hopeful! Great things are ahead of you!

"Matter of fact - insightful - light hearted"

- K.A.S.

Labor of Love

Going through Menopause

is like giving birth to a new you.

You need to go through the labor pains

before you are born once more.

TRAIL
MARKER

"Relatable and a good reminder of what's important."

> - Marianne

"Thought provoking and a reminder of who I want to be."

> - Kimberley

"Raise your words, not your voice.
It is rain that grows flowers, not thunder."

> - Rumi

*%$@#!

Why is it so easy to swear?

Now, mind you, I have been there.

When emotions run high

those words slip out and you look up to the sky

and think "What was that all about?".

It's like something gave them a push

and as much as you wish

you can't reel them back in.

And that is just the thing:

they're gloomy, no good and crude

and truly mirror your attitude.

So, it goes deeper than just a few words.

The question is: 'Who am I ? And how do I

want to be heard?'

With that in mind

I can choose to speak kind

Lift up my head and stand up tall

and tell those words to fall

away to the side of the road

and focus on uplifting words to be sowed.

TRAIL
MARKER

A core of friends with whom a strong bond exists is a true blessing.

Recently, when one of my friends was struggling hard, I hurt with her.

I wanted to hold her, to comfort her, to take away the pain. Tears welled up inside of me and her agony was so acute that I couldn't even find the words to title my emotions.

We each have to walk our paths; yet, the way seems so much brighter and lighter when we have friends walking beside us.

"Love the freedom in these words; the challenge; the acceptance."

- K. Avallon

————————

The pain in your eyes cuts me to the bone

Every tear that falls feels like acid on my soul

I want to take your place

Yet you know I can't

The path is yours

You recognize only you can change its course

That makes me love you even more

Take my time, my love, my regard

Use them as markers, as lights

And let them accompany you

To your destination

TRAIL
MARKER

Breathe

Drop your shoulders

Pick a wonderful memory

One that lifts you up and carries

you to a time of contentment and love

"A harvest of peace is produced from a seed of contentment."

- Proverb

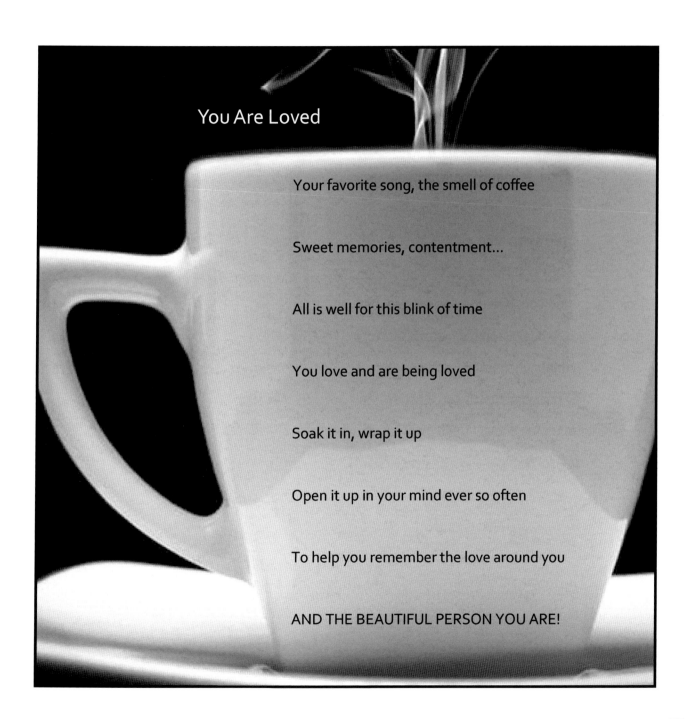

You Are Loved

Your favorite song, the smell of coffee

Sweet memories, contentment...

All is well for this blink of time

You love and are being loved

Soak it in, wrap it up

Open it up in your mind ever so often

To help you remember the love around you

AND THE BEAUTIFUL PERSON YOU ARE!

TRAIL
MARKER

Things don't seem the same anymore.

Between physical changes and emotional surprises I feel like I'm in a free fall.

Acknowledging the new normal as I'm climbing the Mountain of Menopause, I am learning to smile and take one day at a time.

Let's take a break, sit in the grass, and laugh about this crazy and confusing chapter we are passing through.

"Funny... sounds like an episode of 'The Twilight Zone'."

- L. Fox

Where did it go?

A.K.A.

The Body Snatchers

What happened?

Hair appears where there was none,

and disappears where should be some!

The body's bulging here and there.

C'mon, this just isn't fair!

And then the heat, no cold, no heat.

This might seem strange to some...

But those with a similar conundrum

are wondering and contemplating:

where, and by whom their true bodies where taken.

What? How long? You must be joking!

Clear the path,

run me a bath

to do some major soaking!

Around me, the candles will throw a most advantageous light

on this body of mine.

And the world, once again, shall be alright!

TRAIL
MARKER

Keeping joy in tact as we travel through this season can be strenuous.

When people we love and care for rain on our parade, it is even harder.

Yet we must stay the course!

Don't let them take your joy !

"Blaze the trail for positive in your life!"

"Joy does not simply happen to us.
We have to choose joy and keep choosing it every day."

- Henri J.M. Nouwen

Keeping the Joy

Protect the joy inside of you

like an impenetrable fort

Don't let them in

The joy killers

It is by choice

they want to hurt, to push, to stab

Those evil thinkers and long-faced thieves

those pokey-mokers with hurtful deeds

You keep on joy-ing, no matter what

No good will come from joining them

NO -

Joy will spread

there is no doubt

So keep on going

and they just might

participate in your delight

TRAIL
MARKER

When I found myself confused and it seemed
that all my thoughts and emotions where
flying around in one big tornado inside of me,
I encountered this wonderful artist.

He reminded me of my father, of an old friend.
The look in his eyes was peaceful and filled with love.
At that time in my life that was exactly what I was
yearning for: peace.

Peace comes after war, and I realized that I needed to
fight my own battles first.

"Unique - Very insightful"

- Marianne A.

The Rockstar

It was those eyes, not what you do

that made us go and watch you

The place was small

compared to some

yet suited perfectly for what's to come

You were at ease

igniting the air with every piece

Then came the crown

the cherry on top

The time to meet

and time just stopped

Those eyes

beaming with joy and love

showed that time's been tough

yet out of it you chose the path

to share that love

and laugh

It is a choice to shine one's light

so bright

as to illuminate the night for others

who, in the dark

seek that spark

to follow

and help them get through tomorrow

You brighten their day

in the most wonderful way

with your joy, calm, and peace

and inspire them

to get up from their knees

to stare life square in the face

and conquer it

each at their own pace

Now, they're ALL Rockstars

because you cared

and didn't bend

but persevered

following your own course

TRAIL
MARKER

What makes you feel alive?
Is it an adrenaline rush, fear, reaching a goal,
competition?

Being afraid of heights, I feel truly alive when I set foot
on the ground again after a long flight.

What gives you that feeling that makes you so
grateful that you are almost bursting at the seams with
excitement?

When there is nothing you can't do and nobody can
stand in your way.

It is a beautiful thing to feel that alive!

"Because you are alive, anything is possible."

- Thích Nhât Hanh

ALIVE !

To be alive

To feel the gift

To breathe the air

Is such a joy

And privilege

It calms the soul

Yet stirs it too

And makes aware

That time is short

To be held on to

To be alive, to be alive

WHAT A WONDERMENT IT IS

TO BE ALIVE!

Photo Credits

Growing Up.........Tuk Tuk Design

The Gift.......Greg Reese

Morning Appreciation......Hans Braxmeier

Snow.......monicore

The Dog.......Kerstin Schaefer

My Love.........Myicahel Tamburini

Tears.......Fabian Reitmeier

Obstacles.......Mabel Amber

Homecoming.......Claudia Weigelt

Doors........qimono

In the Moment......Kerstin Schaefer

Look......Free-Photos pixabay

YOU......Skitterphoto

*%$@#!......Anna Waldl

Unnamed Poem......Annie Spratt

You Are Loved......skeeze

Where did it go?......Mabel Amber

The Rockstar......Alexa_Fotos